What's That Smell?

by Ximena Hastings
illustrations by Alison Hawkins

Ready-to-Read

SIMON SPOTLIGHT
An imprint of Simon & Schuster Children's Publishing Division
New York   London   Toronto   Sydney   New Delhi
1230 Avenue of the Americas, New York, New York 10020
This Simon Spotlight edition August 2022 • Text copyright © 2022 by Simon & Schuster, Inc.
Illustrations copyright © 2022 by Alison Hawkins • Stock photos by iStock
All rights reserved, including the right of reproduction in whole or in part in any form.
SIMON SPOTLIGHT, READY-TO-READ, and colophon are registered trademarks of Simon & Schuster, Inc.
For information about special discounts for bulk purchases, please contact Simon & Schuster Special Sales at 1-866-506-1949
or business@simonandschuster.com. • Manufactured in the United States of America 0722 LAK • 10 9 8 7 6 5 4 3 2 1
Library of Congress Cataloging-in-Publication Data
Names: Hastings, Ximena, author. | Hawkins, Alison, illustrator.
Title: What's that smell? / by Ximena Hastings ; illustrations by Alison Hawkins.
Description: New York : Simon Spotlight, [2022] | Series: Super gross | Contents: The Power of Noses! — Super Stinky! — Icky, Stinky Body! |
Audience: Ages 5–7 | Audience: Grades K–1 | Summary: "Sniff your way into the world of stinky things in this super fun book in a
nonfiction Level 2 Ready-to-Read series about all the grossest things! This book will focus on some of the stinkiest things on the planet, like
bodily odors, animal smells, and smelly things found in nature"— Provided by publisher.
Identifiers: LCCN 2022013222 (print) | LCCN 2022013223 (ebook) | ISBN 9781665920766 (hardcover) | ISBN 9781665920759 (paperback)
| ISBN 9781665920773 (ebook) Subjects: LCSH: Smell—Juvenile literature. | Nose—Juvenile literature. | Senses and sensation—Juvenile
literature. Classification: LCC QP458 .H335 2022 (print) | LCC QP458 (ebook) | DDC 612.8/6—dc23/20220325
LC record available at https://lccn.loc.gov/2022013222 LC ebook record available at https://lccn.loc.gov/2022013223

Glossary

bacteria: organisms that live in our food or bodies

carbohydrates: types of plant materials that animals eat

cells: small units that make up living things

genetics: the biological features that we get from our parents

olfactory: relating to the sense of smell

poisonous: a material that is very harmful if touched or swallowed

receptor: cells that receive sensations

Note to readers: Some of these words may have more than one definition. The definitions above match how these words are used in this book.

Contents

Chapter 1:
The Power of Noses

Hi there! My name is Dr. Ick.
As my name suggests,
I like all things icky, stinky,
and gross!

This is my good friend, Sam.
He doesn't love stinky things
as much as I do, but as a dog,
he knows *a lot* about them.
We're here to show you some of
the smelliest things in the world!

Did you know that humans can smell some things as well as dogs can?

No way!

Yes way!
Humans can be sensitive
to certain scents.
Some of these specific smells are
bananas, flowers, blood,
and even urine!

7

Some people are so sensitive
to smells, they're called
"super smellers"!

PIZZA!

Some super smellers are born with this ability, but other people can train their noses to become better smellers and use it for work!

That's right, Sam.
Dogs have more **olfactory receptor**
(say: ohl-FAK-tuh-ree rih-SEP-ter)
cells in their noses
than humans do.

That means that dogs' special noses help them pick up more smells, and dogs recognize the scents much more quickly!

Chapter 2: Super Stinky!

What's the first animal
you think of when you hear
the word "stinky"?
If one of your guesses was a skunk,
then you have a good nose!

Skunks can spray as far as twelve feet! That's almost half the width of a tennis net!

Skunks are some of the smelliest
animals on the planet.
When skunks are scared,
they spray something called
musk from their butt!
Some even do it while
doing a handstand!

13

A lot of other animals,
like the stink bug and the
bombardier (say: bahm-buh-DEER)
beetle, also release stinky sprays
when they feel they are in danger.

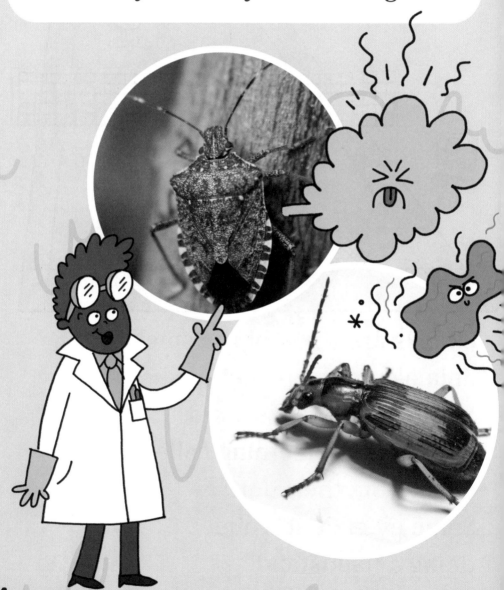

Some animals are smelly
in other interesting ways!
Did you know that bearcat urine
smells like buttered popcorn?

It doesn't just stop at animals, though. There are a lot of smells found in nature! Lemongrass is a plant that got its name by smelling like lemons!

Another plant that smells like its name is the potato bush.
Even though it smells like potatoes, you can't eat it!
It is **poisonous** (say: POY-zuhn-uhs), which means it can harm you.

Not everything that has a strong smell
is dangerous (say: DAYN-juh-ruhs).
In fact, some of my favorite foods
have the strongest smells!

One of them is Limburger cheese.
It's one of the smelliest cheeses
in the world due to the **bacteria**
(say: bak-TEER-ee-uh) used to age it.
Yum!

Chapter 3:
Icky, Stinky Body!

Now I want to show you some of the smelly things inside your body!

The human body is full of interesting smells that live all over us—inside and out! But did you know, the thing that makes us most stinky is bacteria?

Bacteria in our bodies feed on everything, from our food to dead skin cells, and the ways they process those things result in certain smells.

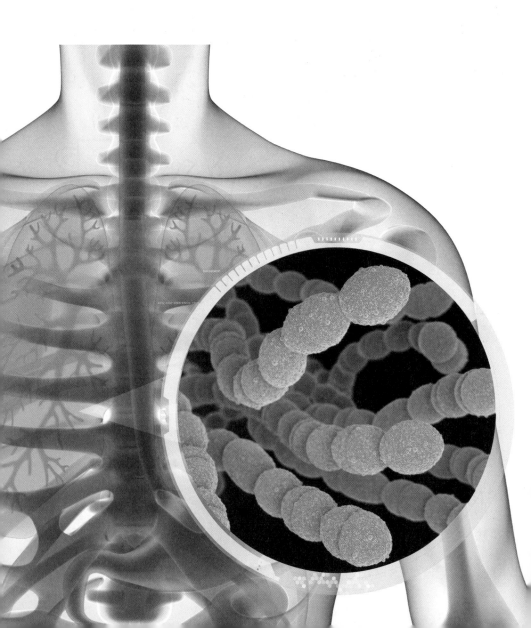

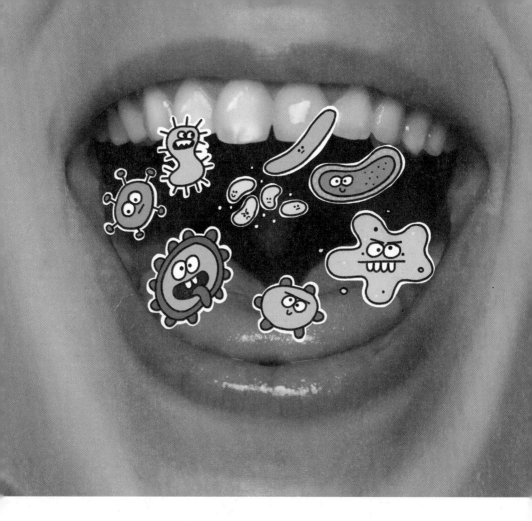

Take your mouth, for example.
After you eat, bacteria break
down your food and then live
inside your mouth!
It isn't until you brush your teeth
or clean your mouth that some
of the bacteria go away.
For a little while, at least!

Have you ever wondered why some people's armpits smell? It's also because of bacteria!

Bacteria like to live in wet, dark places. When you sweat, bacteria gather and can create stinky smells underneath your arms!

Of course, the grossest smell that comes from our body is . . . GAS! Our gas can smell different depending on what we eat.

Foods like broccoli and brussels sprouts are more difficult for our stomachs to break down because they are rich in **carbohydrates** (say: kahr-boh-HIE-drayts). This means that the bacteria have to work hard—making things *extra* stinky!

That's enough about gas! Did you know that different people can actually smell the same thing in different ways?

Some people think the the herb cilantro (say: sih-LAHN-troh) smells like soap. Others smell a strong chemical in their urine after eating asparagus! It all has to do with **genetics** (say: juh-NEH-tiks) and the cells we have in our body.

Isn't it amazing how many
smells there are in the world?
Some scents are delicious,
but some are definitely not!

Even though lots of scents are gross,
certain smells can bring back
happy memories or even
make us laugh!
So go out, take a big whiff, and follow
that nose!

The Stinky Sock Test!

Before you begin this experiment, ask a parent or guardian for help!

Materials Needed:

- A sock
- A strong-smelling liquid, like perfume

Instructions:

How strong is your sense of smell? Take the Stinky Sock Test and find out! Have a grown-up spray a strong-smelling liquid onto a sock and then hide it. Count to twenty and then search for the stinky sock, using your nose as a guide!